TIME TO COMPARE!

Which IS HEAVIER?

first concepts

BY JAGGER YOUSSEF

Gareth Stevens
PUBLISHING

We can compare!
The rock is heavier.

3

The hippo is heavier.

5

The watermelon
is heavier.

7

The red ball
is heavier.

9

The black dog
is heavier.

The blue book
is heavier.

13

The yellow chair
is heavier.

15

The purple truck
is heavier.

17

The green bag
is heavier.

Two blocks
are heavier
than one.

21

Point to the
heavier bear.

23

Please visit our website, www.garethstevens.com. For a free color catalog of all our high-quality books, call toll free 1-800-542-2595 or fax 1-877-542-2596.

Library of Congress Cataloging-in-Publication Data
 Names: Youssef, Jagger, author.
Title: Which is heavier? / Jagger Youssef.
Description: New York : Gareth Stevens Publishing, [2021] | Series: Time to
  compare! | Includes index.
Identifiers: LCCN 2019043409 | ISBN 9781538254967 (library binding) | ISBN
  9781538254943 (paperback) | ISBN 9781538254950 (6 Pack) | ISBN 9781538254974
  (ebook)
Subjects: LCSH: Weight (Physics)–Measurement–Juvenile literature. |
  Weight judgment–Juvenile literature. | Comparison (Psychology) in
  children–Juvenile literature.
Classification: LCC QC106 .Y68 2021 | DDC 530.8–dc23
LC record available at https://lccn.loc.gov/2019043409

First Edition

Published in 2021 by
Gareth Stevens Publishing
111 East 14th Street, Suite 349
New York, NY 10003

Designer: Sarah Liddell
Editor: Therese Shea

Photo credits: Cover, p. 1 (main) Elena Sherengovskaya/Shutterstock.com; cover, p. 1 (background) oksanka007/ Shutterstock.com; p. 3 (marble) Photo Melon/Shutterstock.com; p. 3 (rock) nasidastudio/Shutterstock.com; p. 5 (hippo) Eric Isselee/Shutterstock.com; p. 5 (mouse) Rudmer Zwerver/Shutterstock.com; p. 7 (apple) Tim UR/Shutterstock. com; p. 7 (watermelon) Maks Narodenko/Shutterstock.com; p. 9 (bowling ball) Mega Pixel/Shutterstock.com; p. 9 (tennis ball) Kapustin Igor/Shutterstock.com; p. 11 (brown dog) Andrey_Kuzmin/Shutterstock.com; p. 11 (black dog) ARTSILENSE/Shutterstock.com; p. 13 (blue book) Funny Solution Studio/Shutterstock.com; p. 13 (red book) piccatcher/ Shutterstock.com; p. 15 (yellow chair) Ksana Durand/Shutterstock.com; p. 15 (green chair) design56/Shutterstock. com; p. 17 (white truck) Adisa/Shutterstock.com; p. 17 (purple truck) Rob Wilson/Shutterstock.com; p. 19 (brown bag) Susan Schmitz/Shutterstock.com; p. 19 (green bag) Billion Photos/Shutterstock.com; p. 21 (two blocks) Shavel Aksana/ Shutterstock.com; p. 21 (one block) HeinzTeh/Shutterstock.com; p. 23 (teddy bear) aldegonde/Shutterstock.com; p. 23 (brown bear) Daria Rybakova/Shutterstock.com.

Printed in the United States of America

Some of the images in this book illustrate individuals who are models. The depictions do not imply actual situations or events.

CPSIA compliance information: Batch #CS20GS: For further information contact Gareth Stevens, New York, New York at 1-800-542-2595.

Find us on